Structural Steel Industrial Business Management

Structural Steel Industrial Business Management

A Hand book for the structural
steel Fabricators, manufactures,
management specialist, consultants

Saji Thomas

Copyright © 2011 by Saji Thomas.

ISBN: Softcover   978-1-4691-3500-7
           Ebook   978-1-4691-3501-4

All rights reserved. No part of this book may be reproduced or transmitted in any form or by any means, electronic or mechanical, including photocopying, recording, or by any information storage and retrieval system, without permission in writing from the copyright owner.

This is a work of fiction. Names, characters, places and incidents either are the product of the author's imagination or are used fictitiously, and any resemblance to any actual persons, living or dead, events, or locales is entirely coincidental.

This book was printed in the United States of America.

To order additional copies of this book, contact:
Xlibris Corporation
1-888-795-4274
www.Xlibris.com
Orders@Xlibris.com

PREFACE

This book is the result of my field experience in structural steel industry, when I am doing different role in a large manufacturing company I have experienced many challenges. There are various causes for every issue's that arises in structural steel industrial business and to tackle the issues every minute is a real challenge. I have dealt about management, operation, fabrication process and IT role importance in structural steel manufacturing business.

A stage after improvement or expansion in structural steel a well systematic approach and control is must to run the business efficiently with the objectives. Functional organization and its activities defining up to the level of recording macro information which supports to plan the production and delivery IT supported management is unavoidable. The aim to utilize time and resources, the importance of functional integration is the core of the management to maximize utilization, resources and control cost operation.

This book gives functions required for the structural steel business management to execute an operation, manufacturing process and needed module for the structural steel business.

Thanks
Saji Thomas

CONTENTS

1. Management — 1
   a. Overview about structural steel industry — 1
   b. Structural steel Industry and Management — 3
   c. Functions of structural steel Industry — 4
2. Estimation Management — 5
   a. Quantity takeoff methods — 5
   b. Cost estimate general structure for structural steel — 6
   c. Major challenges of structural steel estimate — 7
3. Planning Management — 9
   a. Work breakdown structure for Scheduling — 9
   b. Major area to get schedule interruptions — 10
   c. Role of the planning management — 12
4. Project Management — 14
   a. Scope Management — 15
   b. Communication management — 15
   c. Time Management — 16
   d. Cost Management — 17
   e. Costing — 17
   f. Billing — 18
   g. Claim & Risk Management — 19
   h. Integration Management — 20
   i. Monitor Project Execution — 21
   j. Project closing — 22
5. Engineering — 23
   a. Engineering Management — 24
   b. Communication — 24
6. Material Management — 26
   a. Objectives of Inventory Management and Control — 26
   b. Inventory Classification — 26

	c.	Optimum inventory	27
	d.	Inventory Management	27
	e.	Optimum Inventory Levels	27
	f.	Degree to Control	28
	g.	Inventory Control Systems	28
	h.	Basic Communication Forms	29
	i.	Material Management common function in structural steel industry	29
	j.	Material Requirement Planning	30
	k.	Procurement process	30
	l.	Shipping	30
	m.	Material receiving, storage, issuance and control scrap	31
7.	Manufacturing	32
	a.	Manufacturing Functions	32
	b.	Production Planning & control	32
	c.	Manufacturing Preparation process	33
	d.	Manufacturing fabrication process	33
	e.	Blasting / surface preparation process	33
	f.	Painting / Galvanizing process	34
	g.	Plant maintenance	34
	h.	Structural steel Fabrication sequences of activities	34
	i.	Welding	40
	j.	Residual welding stresses	42
	k.	Control of distortion	43
	l.	Methods of correcting distortion	43
	m.	Defects in welds	44
8.	Quality Control	46
	a.	Quality control Focus in structural steel industry	47
	b.	Process inspection stages	47
	c.	Quality control in fabrication	48
9.	Major challenge or constraints of operations	51
10.	IT role for structural steel business	52
11.	Conclusion	54

MANAGEMENT

Overview about structural steel industry

For every organization or even family, management is basic key for the execution and success of anything. Management is the process of activities getting completed efficiently and effectively with and through other people. Management and its functional execution performance is an important role to success the structural steel business. In structural steel business a generalized management method may not be enough, functions have its own specialty and priority. If we look in to structural steel management the complexity of the management in terms of handling functions are high in a mass production location. In structural steel mass production definition varies from other industry. Assume a company who produce just 500MT of standard structural steel for more than one customer, its operation mode moves to mass production may be you're surprising now. Producing one tone of structural steel minimum of 68 operation just to do in production line. Look at the below table:-

Assume for one ton consist of 4 pieces of 250kg which have 4 templates for assembly in normal case:-

Activity for finishing one piece of 250kg	
Process	No of operation
Preparation	5
Fitting	4
Welding	4
Blasting	1
Painting	1
Inspection	1
Packing	1
No of stages passed for one piece	17
Total number of stages required to pass for one tone	68

The above illustration is only for production line, in engineering detailing, materials procurement not considered. In case in detailing stage if any missing connection details, after the fabrication drawing if any revision, these all unusual events are common in structural steel industrial business. So in quantity wise structural steel could not classify. Going back to manage structural steel sophisticated positions are not so important but functional integration, knowledge of the operation and personal dedication is highly important.

Let us assume an organization where they have the capacity to produce an average of 6000 – 8000 ton of structural steel their type of management set-up for the business. How to set-up a standard functional management, it is not so mandatory, according to the organization and nature of the government policy also directly linked. But some of functions are common and important for the structural steel industry. In structural steel business certain functions and its way of management have high value since this business output almost all the cases are controlled by time. Where the business is controlled by time each minute of operation should be recorded with concerned activity and measuring in terms of money. In each functions every hours status of the functions are keep-on changing due to many factors it may be minor or it may be major, regardless either minor or major if the information not reached in to the right person outcome either it will be missed or things to be re do when the realization minute. More than the number of designation of management functions and its prompt execution are very important in any business. When it goes to structural steel industrial manufacturing function's prompt execution linked with time and money.

Major function of structural steel industries off-course sales, marketing and business development is one of the business function there is no doubt about it and it is also an important function of structural steel industry. But in structural steel industry market and forecast depending various as aspect of the other industries. And it has also direct relation with the performance of structural steel manufacturer. Some case if a best performer of the structural steel manufacturer can work as like permanent supplier for their customer without putting high investment in marketing. There are two major factors influencing structural steel market one is delivery promptness and second one is price. To support sales, marketing and business development function in order to have a face other functions proper execution is vital even though the complexity is high.

Structural steel Industry and Management

Structural steel business is one of the wide scope of industrial business for the present and future. In order to run structural steel business effectively there are many internal operational challenges rather than facing market competition. In this book I am mainly dealing for the management to face the operational challenges.

I have seen structural steel manufacturing Company were facing everyday many issues in production, claims, commitment to the customer not delivering, budgeted output not meeting for the management. This may be common issues in structural steel industry but its impact affecting the business.

In a global view the management and execution of the structural steel production is nothing it is easy can be done without any harm according to the demand of the customer. Some of the companies who are actively involved the market incase sometimes its performance goes down more than the tolerable level of the management, from that point to bring in to a stable line of the flow companies takes years. There are many constraints depending to run this business in streamline. The word constraints have two meaning in structural steel industry one is easy to identify and other one is not easy to identify. Major users of the structural steel products, they have the assumption that once engineering design part done the scope of the structural steel manufacture to do the detailing one side and procure the raw-materials based on earlier schedule and go for the fabrication, coating and delivery. Yes if the flow works this way structural steel industrial business will become easy and can run the business in stable condition. Let me explain my point of view to identify challenge and how to overcome it for the structural steel industrial business.

The following are the major functions of structural steel business management:-

Functions of structural steel Industry

- Estimation
- Planning
- Project Management
- Engineering
- Materials Planning
- Manufacturing
- Quality control

When you define the management for your business it is not necessary to have each function should work as an independent department or sections. In any organization especially to manage and control cost, efficient way of functional design will be playing major role. In structural steel industry a highly integrated system of management is mandatory from the starting point to generation of invoicing. Integration in micro level of business and process to be define in a powerful database for the functional execution. It will help to reduce the complexity of management and operation and will help to work the functions efficiently and cost effectively. For the best way of the operation regardless of any capacity an integrated management system is unavoidable in structural steel business.

ESTIMATION MANAGEMENT

Estimation of structural steel can be a complex activity because of the variety of members, member size, applications, fabrication requirements, detailing and connection types. Erection methods, equipment used, and project conditions also play significant roles in pricing of structural steel. Accurate estimation of structural steel requires specialized knowledge of fabrication and erection methods.

The estimation management has to review thoroughly about the project plan, specification, contractual condition, project site condition and correlate the information, accordingly should prepare work break down structure to illustrate the elements which will need to be addressed the detailed estimate. And the items for which to seek lower tier sub-contractors or suppliers example steel joists, metal decking, steel grating etc. will be purchased for the project from suppliers. Will need to determine whether the steel need to procure from steel rolling mill, steel service provider or own inventory.

Quantity takeoff methods

Estimator must undertake a very careful quantity takeoff of each separate element with its corresponding shape and size for the steel. Each shape, bolt, clip etc. will need to be accounted. Beams and columns will typically be recorded separately because the fabrication requirements for these components will vary. In addition, the connections, fabrication, material characteristics, weld requirements and finishing requirements for each member will need to be identified and tallied. Because of the complexity of this risk a systematic methods for taking off steel will be an advantages. The estimator should review all plans, including the structural, architectural and mechanical sheets. All documents should be correlated to obtain a complete understanding of the project, including administrative and procedural requirements. Because architects and engineers have individual style of organizing information on the plans, the estimator must quickly adapt to the symbols, sheet arrangement and level of detail on the set of plans being worked with. A useful in structuring the takeoff is to develop a master checklist or a work break-down structure (WBS).

Connections for the various members will have a significant impact on fabrication and material costs, therefore each connection will need to be described and designed. In addition to the main members other steel item which is attached to the frame such as bracing, angle, bent plates, framing for roof or floor etc. these elements can add considerable fabrication time as well as tonnage for the project. In addition miscellaneous loose structural steel items and metal fabrications also to be listed so estimator must carefully review the architectural, structural and mechanical sheets.

Cost estimate general structure for structural steel

a. Cost including applicable tax, custom duty from mill, service provider or inventory
b. Freight for shipping materials from the mill or warehouse to the fabricator's plant
c. Cost of preparing shop and erection drawings, including engineering if required printing and distribution
d. Cost of fabrication of the structural steel elements, including connections and special processes such as bending or cambering etc..
e. Finishing the members, including surface cleaning, painting or galvanizing

f. Cost of independent testing
g. Handling, storage and loading cost at the fabrication plant
h. Field verification and surveying anchor rod locations
i. Shop testing and inspection
j. Shop expense including general overhead, supervision, plant and equipment etc..
k. Freight for shipping fabricated element to the project site
l. Product liability insurance
m. Bonds
n. Subcontracted items such as steel grating, metal deck, handrail etc..
o. General administration overhead

Major challenges of structural steel estimate

Even though steel estimates done on the bases of cost of materials, detailing, approvals, fabrication, finishing, delivery as well as administrative procedures, profit and overhead. The cost associated with fabrication will not be impacted by amount of material but also the type of material and shape called in the design as well as complexity of the connection and other fabrications. The steel estimator must be skilled at qualifying and characterizing each piece of steel for the project. The following are the major concentrate given for structural steel estimate

1. Raw-material Procurement
2. Material type and strength
3. Shop drawing & approvals
4. Fabrication and connections
5. Fabrication capacity and shop operation
6. Painting and finishing
7. Inspection
8. Loading, storage, delivery and transportation
9. Special Buy-out Items

To have the best pricing definition, its function has to be defined the flow of the management. Some company's execution department naming estimation section, some companies this function organizing as a part of engineering department, some companies it will be part of sales department function, it can be related function of engineering or it can make as separate independent section for costing and product pricing. The function involves engineering as well as costing aspect of the business. A detailed analysis to be covered from the available data by adopting learned lesions, engineering, previous experience, process costing, type of the work to be carried out its specification, testing & inspection all these data has to manage carefully for the structural steel costing. More over future execution package details and its reference should maintain.

In structural steel cost estimation is not so easy, at the time of the bidding level many information may not be available and the time constraint for the bid. Some case customer provide only main sections, some cases few sample bid drawing, usually most of the cases very few information about the project only available. Since it is the initial budgeting stage to manage the project so all the unforeseen or maximum unusual events has to cover as mentioned. Operation complexity covering is one the major challenge, all the case complexity could not identify at the initial stage of the bid, the reason detailed engineering data won't available. Such situation to cover either with previous experience of the same project in this case historical data must be recorded in your data base.

Product categorization of pricing commonly defined like heavy, medium, light steel order but its identity with product name and size will be give advantage to the business and convince for the department operation. Most convenient mode for the measure of structural steel estimation can be done in terms of tone or support product area wise. Every calculation is based on time for the process, so the complexity part of the project initially may not clear this is usual hidden risk of structural steel, to cover this type of hidden risk estimator should take additional precaution in the line of his estimate. Here historical or personal experience will help to determine certain extend but again actual time recording in each part of the structural member not so important and it is too difficult task even for the all process but sub-package assembly level maintaining will help the estimation.

PLANNING MANAGEMENT

In order to make an effective and practical schedule for the execution of the overall project, the planner or scheduler should understand the role and responsibilities of the participants impact the schedule. A careful coordination plan has to set-up for all the primary activities:-

1. Get MTO & Process Order
2. Produce erection drawings
3. Produce shop drawings
4. Fabrication
5. Quality Control
6. Delivery
7. Coordinate Delivery for SBO
8. Coordinate Delivery for miscellaneous steel

Work breakdown structure for Scheduling

WBS is the starting point for the development of a detailed plan for the project and has to break in different component parts to increasingly lower levels. This breakdown is continued until the project is fully defined in terms of activities and it is considered in terms of time and resources. The following is a sample method for the structural activity and durations:-

Sr. No	Activity Descriptions	Duration	Comments
1	Material Quantity Surveying		
2	Material Ordering		
3	Material Receiving, Storage		
4	Material Allocation		
5	Preparation for shop drawing details		
6	Shop drawing approval		
7	Shop drawing & BOM releases to Shop		
8	Material Issue		
9	Fabrication		
10	Finishing		
12	Delivery		

Major area to get schedule interruptions

The following are the major area to get schedule interruptions so it required high attention and monitoring:-

1. Delays due to non-availability of materials
    a. Material arrival delay from mill
    b. Shortage of materials
    c. Production Delay
    d. Uncommon size / types
    e. Delivery Delay
2. Limitation of Fabrication Shop capacity

a. Machine break-down
   b. Delay of earlier project
   c. Man-power shortage
   d. Strikes
   e. Material shape / complexity
   f. Special inspection / Testing requirements
3. Limitation of Engineering Capacity
   a. Delay of receiving IFC drawing
   b. Revisions, RFI delay of response
   c. Delay of earlier project
   d. Man-power shortage
4. Limitations of Finishing
   a. Special surface requirements
   b. Special coating requirements
   c. Inspection
   d. Earlier project delay
   e. Man-power shortage
   f. Raw-material availability
5. Transportation
   a. Material shape
   b. Packing Delay
   c. Local Civil permit approval
   d. Loading Equipment availability
   e. Over booked
   f. Government / political issues
   g. Financial clearance for delivery

Planning role in structural steel business is very high again it is so complicated and difficult function when it is in structural steel planning point of view. Planning controls sales as well as the entire function of the business. This is the point functional integration takes place to clear the traffic of the operations and ensuring monthly target of the business achieving. Planning management act as the controller of other function, there are many uncertain event will be occurring in structural steel business these type of unexpected event makes many interruption of various function and resources utilization.

Role of the planning management

1. Define process
   Identify and define process is the basic key for planning in structural steel business execution. There are process, stages and flow. Every small or big operation there is time requirement for it. Since structural business most of the case (99.99%) production runs on the bases of time. Every process, stage and flow required time for its own completion or end. It is the tedious task to set time for the process or stage or flow, there is no standard time defined or established for it but it is role of the planning management to define the required time for the completion. Production & engineering are the major resources but some cases like depending external things these stages also to be considered in your planning example raw-material arrival, design drawing availability.

2. Locate data source
   Find right data source, availability and bring it in planning management is very important to measure accuracy & quantity planning in structural steel. Data source to be receive from project management, materials, engineering and production. Some case duplication of data mislead planning. So data source identity and its control should be one of the important thing to avoid duplication.

3. Update information
   Time to time each of the information must be updated for all the process, stage and flow. The important of recording information for planning helps it in project. Like RFI, some case customer will do respond but some case may be responded but it may not communicated or not reached to the right person, this type of incidents are common in this business. Other requests like material substitution its approval to be recorded. All these case there is time consumption, without the response from customer its next stage of action could not proceeds.

4. Define schedule
   Olden times planning means define schedule for the process and organize resource accordingly to object for the target. It is right but in dealing structural steel when it goes for mass production just defining a schedule

won't help. Each project has its own commitment, so to manage smoothly, plan process wise and organize to run process wise. For the functional management schedule is the basic guide line for the operation and also this one of the major outcome of planning management.

5. Track & record progress
   Track and record each process progress on time will able to report the status of the process. Tracking and record to be linked from engineering, materials and production. A real time tracking process will help to monitor and follow-up the activities. It is very important for the planning and controlling the functions

6. Monitor the process
   As a controller of the operation a micro level monitoring has to perform by planning management. It is the source to give input for the next stage of operation as well as to find the alternate solution in case if any variation of the scheduled activity. Monitor each stage, process and flow on real time need for structural steel industry operation because a small information missing will affect major operation and it may cause to vary the schedule, some case it may make big impact financially.

7. Expedite functions
   Expedition is one of the common function of any planning management the same here in structural steel industry also. Expedition is paying cost if there is no integrated planning management. Independent or just functional wise expedition may not be efficient, example cases like material arrival date from mill, specified section placed order was cancelled or customer have put a hold for that particular section, or customer have revised the design etc.. all these type of events to be tracked and then only expedition will work in structural steel.

8. Manage to achieve target
   All the above exercise should result to achieve the target this is outcome of the planning for all the business. In structural steel because of many depending stages achieve a planned target is one of the major challenge. A well-integrated plan in each stage, flow and process wise is must and it will bring good result and could help to achieve the target.

PROJECT MANAGEMENT

Project management in structural steel industry counted as one of the process owner to execute several functions of the business. Basically project management is the interface between customer and in-house operations. After the purchase order or contract signed by customer remaining activity will be taking by project management this is common in structural steel industry. The major function of the project management is to manage the project efficiently and make maximum revenue for the business. Efficiency of Project management makes the project success and ensuring customer satisfaction. Defining and setting-up project management function in structural industry most cases depends the strategy of the executive management.

Role of Project management in structural steel industry even though it is a customer support executive for the business but there are many functions involved mainly contract analysis, communication, coordination, follow-up and execution monitoring. Project management role not limiting with some of the function but to manage the entire project is the key responsibility. When it deals about project management is very vast but to manage there are specified activities which is vital and key for the management. In structural steel industry project management is source to maintain customer satisfaction and customer relationship. There are many functions involved in structural steel project management by comparing other industries some of the important functions:-

Some of the Important functions of Project Management

Scope Management

Scope Management is the collection of processes which ensure that the project includes all the work required to complete it while excluding all work which is not necessary to complete it. The Scope Management Plan details how the project scope will be defined, developed, and verified. It clearly defines who is responsible for managing the projects' scope and acts as a guide for managing and controlling the scope.

Project scope management involves major five steps:-

a. Collect Requirement
b. Define Scope
c. Create WBS (work break-down structure)
d. Control scope
e. Verify scope

Some companies it is calling contract information Form (CIF), even in whatever name you call as soon as when the contract signing ceremony over next important stage is to hand over it to project management. There first step project management has to analysis and define the scope of the project, it has to go in very details.

Communication management

Communication not only keeps everyone up-to-date on the project progress, but also facilitates to make right decisions in right time and helps to success of the project. To ensure the success of a project much information, including expectations, goals, needs, resources, status reports, budgets and purchase requests, needs to be communicated on a regular basis to the concerned project key members of other functional group.

Usually in structural steel project communication recipients both external and internal there are many parties involving, setting a common channel is difficult. But establish a communication under one single sever is important for the success of the project. To make a communication table organize and list all project term of internal and external on the bases of functions, give group name. To setting a generalized communication method for project management we can form a system as follows in a line order

Communication Item, Communication accountability, objective, recipients

Communication item: This category describes which piece of information need to be communicated.

Accountability: Name of the team member responsible for ensuring such communication occurs.

Objective: It intends what specific objective you will accomplish by delivering it.

Recipients: It describes which person or groups will be receiving intended communication

Time Management

When you know how to manage your time you gain control. Rather than busily working here, there, and everywhere (and not getting much done anywhere), effective time management helps you to choose what to work on and when. This is essential if you're to achieve anything of any real worth. In structural steel business time directly linked with sales so managing time is highly depending for the success of the project. To manage time efficiently and utilize the time effectively the following measures effectively need to do

1. Setting-up priority
2. Make a common activity log
3. Create schedules

Cost Management

In structural steel industry costing and billing most of the companies are controlling by project management. As soon as project awarded sales and estimation functional will handover contract details and estimated data to project management to carry out further activities of the project. Project billing is the responsibility of the project management according to the progress of the process and shipments / delivery.

Costing

Even though estimated cost data existing for the project, actual cost management will take place from project management. Cost Estimating is the process of developing an approximation of the cost of the resources needed to complete project activities including the consideration of the possible fluctuations and other variances such as risk. Throughout the Cost Estimating process various alternatives are considered to assure accurate and effective estimates. This process is conjoined with the Activity Resource Estimating process and is foundational work necessary for Cost Budgeting. The inputs to the cost estimating process are outputs from the other planning processes. These include the project scope statement, the project management plan, the work breakdown structure, staffing management plan, enterprise environmental factors, and organizational process assets. The main outputs of the cost estimating process are the Activity Cost Estimates and the Activity Cost Estimate Supporting Detail.

- **Activity Cost Estimates** -These are assessments of the probable costs of the resources necessary to complete project activities.
- **Activity Cost Estimate Supporting Detail** - This provides a description of the activity's scope of work, documentation about how the estimate was developed, known constraints, explanations of any assumptions that were made, and a range of possible results.

Two additional outputs of the Cost Estimating process are Requested Changes and Cost Management Plan (updates), which incorporate desired and approved changes that are believed to have an impact on the project's cost management.

Cost budgeting is the process of aggregating the estimated costs of individual activities or work packages to establish a cost baseline. It requires having all cost estimating processes completed. The difference between cost estimates and a cost budget is that the cost estimates portray costs by category, versus a cost budget which displays costs across time. The inputs into the Cost Budgeting process are:

- **Activity Cost Estimates** - These predict the cost for the project work.
- **Activity Cost Supporting Detail** - This provides useful data on how the estimate came about.
- **Project Schedule and the Resource Calendar** - Both dictate when project activities occur and when associated budget monies will be spent.
- **The Contract** This details purchasing requirements and associated cost.
- **The Cost Management Plan** -This reflects how project costs will be controlled.
  The end result of the Cost Budgeting process is a Cost Baseline, which is a time-phased budget that will be used to measure and monitor overall cost performance on the project—usually displayed in the form of an S-curve. Additionally, the Cost Budgeting process will produce Project Funding Requirements, including a management reserve amount that is included along with the cost baseline to compensate for either early progress or cost overruns.

To make this function easy and to have better control, integration with estimation, project management, purchasing and finance will simplify its complexity.

Billing

Project billing is one of major function of project management. To do better billing project categorization definition should implement in engineering bill of materials. Structural steel base data is bill of materials all the operation depends directly to the bill of materials. Progressive billing will need to do as per the contract and billing against delivery it will be based on your actual packing list, whatever category given in your purchase order should reflect under the scope management form should be integrated with engineering bill of materials. Structural steel billing is sensitive when you do major project.

Claim & Risk Management

In structural steel business is one of highly dependency type of business example you have to depend customer for the MTO, IFC drawing, shop drawing the same way need to depend supplier like rolling mills for steel raw-material, consumable. One side risk factors are high in structural steel business and other side positive claim and negative claims chance are also equally standing. The success of the project depends, how efficiently managing these events clearly in right time. Project management should give high focus to manage risk, the following are the major ways commonly using for risk:-

Risk Analysis commonly using in project management

    a. Risk identification
    b. Contract and specification requirements
    c. Disaster prevention and relief planning
    d. Probability Analysis
    e. Materializing Review
    f. Sensitivity Analysis
    g. Modeling Risk Profiles
    h. Request for Information (RFI) assessment
    i. Cost escalation analysis
    j. Risk monitoring
    k. Schedule & cost forecasting
    l. Delay & Disruption
    m. Damage Assessment

Claim Management:

In structural steel business there are positive and negative claims both are equally powerful. Some case this is the source to make the project positive as well as excellent gain for the business. Even well managing project will encounter many events which is beneficial for the business, like engineering design change, later stage engineering revisions, delay to get material list, client approvals, specification change the same way there are negative claims like due to poor performance of production, engineering, material procurement delay, materials missing or damage. To perform claims project management handling staff efficiency, knowledge and management set-up also depends. Methods to manage claims:-

Methods to manage claims

a. Determining liability: identification analysis and evaluation of the factual and contractual issues to determine liability.
b. Establishing cost: Performing delay, acceleration and productivity analyses to determine the effect of the action or inaction of the responsible parties on time and cost
c. Calculating Damage: Determine the monetary cost of damages resulting from the contractors or designer's actions and inactions and whether these damages are reasonable, allowable, provable, and recoverable
d. Resolving claims: Based upon its proven track record, project management should do negotiations, arbitration, litigation, or administrative hearings necessary to develop and satisfy resolution to claim.

To handling risk and claim most of the fabricators facing difficulties and small scale fabricators may not having the facility to track such issues.

Integration Management

Many of the structural steel business running there is no integration of their functional operations. Its impact severally affecting in terms of business growth, financial lose, unhealthy management. Most of the companies personal dependency is high because of missing integration, personal dependency have limit a certain extend after will lose confident of all the functional executives and will stop the growth of the business.

Integration Management includes the processes and activities needed to identify, define, combine, unify, and coordinate the various processes and project management activities within the Project Management Process Groups. In the project management context, integration includes characteristics of unification, consolidation, articulation, and integrative actions that are crucial to project completion, successfully meeting customer and other stakeholder requirements and managing expectations. Integration, in the context of managing a project, is making choices about where to concentrate resources and effort on any given day, anticipating potential issues, dealing with these issues before they become critical, and coordinating work for the overall project good.

Monitor Project Execution

Structural steel project monitoring during execution is very important. From the stage of contract receiving from sales, project administration responsibility starts in project management. Establishment of ITP (Inspection Test Program), material list, Engineering design, detailing, approvals, production releases, materials, production progress, revisions, delays etc.. are the common process of structural steel each of the process have many child process. Monitoring and controlling the processes used to initiate, plan, execute, and close a project to meet the performance objectives defined in the project management plan.

Methods used to monitor projects:-

   a. Scope verification
   b. Perform quality control
   c. Manage project team
   d. Performs reporting
   e. Manage customers
   f. Risk monitoring and control
   g. Contract administration

Project closing

Project closing is a tedious job of project management. There are many things to settle this stage like claims, documentations, contract specified items final delivery like QC documents, guarantee certificates, erection drawings submissions. Final step of the closing process will then typically involve transfer, acceptance and approval of the final deliverables to assigning party. It is essential to fully complete the closing process at the conclusion of a project and there are multiple reasons for doing so. First, it assures that, from a financial standpoint, a project is considered closed and that no further charges can be accrued by or attributed to that project. Secondly, it makes it clear to the employer that the project has ended, allowing them to reassign staff and faculty who were previously assigned to that project to another task or activity.

ENGINEERING

In structural steel engineering is the main key for the project production and delivery on time schedule. There are many factors depending in structural steel engineering same like other functions. Most of the case engineering design is out the scope from structural steel manufacturer. Usually engineering starts from detailing and connection design.

Fabricator is responsible for preparing erection drawings that shows piece marks and where the various steel members are to be installed on the job site. These drawings are produced before or simultaneously with the fabrication shop drawings. Erection drawings are also used during shop drawing approval process in order the exact location of the particular member. Shop drawings with details, dimension and location of bolts and welds are necessary for fabrication. Shop drawings provide the instruction that the shop will follow to fabricate the steel. Shop drawing preparation and approval is an important stage. Defective or incomplete shop drawings create significant problems and time delays during fabrication and erection. The main stage to be accounted:-

1. Production
2. Submission
3. Approval

Engineering Management

The basic data creation is done in engineering for the functional production process. This is one of the basic concepts of engineering. List of components that make up a structure will listed in BOM (Bill of Materials). An integrated production system BOM connected the entire operations of the business. Major integrating required area for production:-

1. CNC (Computer Numeric Control): CNC data preparation for the machines which is using for manufacturing process to cut, drills, shape the pieces of materials.

2. Material Optimization: The efficient way to reduce material wastage and maximize utilization of on-hand inventory by using the optimizer

3. Material allocation: In order to create right inventory for the production material allocation has to be integrated with BOM

4. Machine routing: To route the operation required for each pieces for the production

5. Production Schedule: To define each process and progress of the manufacturing

6. Category & Invoice: To define material category, price and integrate PO category

Communication

In order to track, control drawing and engineering data a well-disciplined communication method has to be maintained between the consultant or designer, detailer, programmers. There are many technical clarification may arise while detailing and fabrication. The following are the few methods to handling:-

1. Request for information: This method can be used to get clarification

and clearance for detailing or connection design from customer, consultant or designer etc...

2. Engineering Progress Tracking: Progress for the shop drawing preparation, detailing, revision, information, completion plan up to shop drawing releases.

3. Engineering clarification request: While fabrication if any missing of information or any difficulty for fabrication this method can use for the systematic way to log those shop clarifications.ww

MATERIAL MANAGEMENT

Objectives of Inventory Management and Control

The ultimate objective of all manufacturing controls is to realize a profit through the operation of the business. A more restricted objective of the control of material is to satisfy the customer by meeting the schedule for deliveries. Failure of delivering order on time is one principal cause of loss of business and customers. Effective control of the material throughout the manufacturing cycle reduces the chance of this problem arising.

Material must wait for machines or materials handling equipment to become available and must be ordered in advance of production and stored in a warehouse or storage area.

Inventory Classification

We identify the various functions in material management with the flow of goods, we can identify the different types of inventories or stocks of material maintained in a manufacturing plant. All plants use the same general classification of inventories, including

    a. Raw material
    b. Purchased parts

c. Work-in-progress
   d. Finished goods
   e. Supplies

Optimum inventory

The complex relationship between modern industry and its market presents a real problem in the size of inventories that should be maintained. Large inventories in the face of declining sales mean lower profits. Small and inadequate inventories in the face of an increasing market demand may result in the loss of sales to competitors – and a decreased profit.

Inventory Management

The planning of the control of inventory can be divided into two phases, inventory management and inventory control. Inventory management accomplishes the first phase, consisting of:

1. Determination of optimum inventory levels and procedures for their review and adjustment
2. Determination of the degree of control that is required for the best results
3. Planning and design of the inventory control system
4. Planning of the inventory control organization.

Optimum Inventory Levels

Inventory management is responsible for determining the inventory level that will result in the best profit. But this is not the only factor that must be considered by inventory management when determining inventory levels.

The planning for the actual production of the product may involve problems of leveling production that is producing at a constant rate even though sales may fluctuate. In slack times products are built to stock; the finished goods inventory is increased to offset the demand anticipated when future sales surpass the production rate of the plant. The proper evaluation of this factor requires close cooperation with the manufacturing function.

Degree to Control

Inventory management must decide just how much control is needed to accomplish the objective. The least control – as evidenced by systems, records, and personnel- that is required to perform the function efficiently is the best control. This problem of the degree of control can be approached from the viewpoint of quantity, location and time.

Inventory Control Systems

Control of manufacturing inventories is basically a problem of industrial communications. Earlier, we indicated that the complexity of these systems is directly proportional to the number of items in the inventories and to the number of transactions that have to be recorded to keep abreast of the movement of the material.

The basic information normally carried on perpetual inventory records includes:

1. On order. This part of the record shows the quantity of material ordered but not received. Now order are added in this column and receipts subtracted.
2. Received. All receipts are posted here; there is no balance quantity in this column.
3. On hand. This balance figure represents the quantity of the item that should be in the stock room. Receipts are added to this column and issues subtracted.
4. Issued. A record of all quantities issued to the factory is entered in this column.
5. Allocated. In this column are entered the quantities to be reserved for later issue for specific order. Reserving of materials still in this

stock room will ensure their availability when they are needed on the manufacturing floor.
6. Available. This is the quantity of material "on hand" that is still available for assignment to future orders.

Basic Communication Forms

The basic communication forms used in perpetual inventory control are:

1. Purchase Requisition. This form is prepared by inventory control when new quantities of material should be ordered.
2. Shop order. This form is prepared by inventory control when quantities of material need to be made by the shop for stock.
3. Receiving reports. These are the records of material received by the stock room.
4. Stores requisition. This form authorizes the issuance of any class of inventory material from a controlled storage to the shop. These requisitions may be prepared by the production planner (as we well discuss under production control) or by foremen, supervisor, or other authorized personnel.

Structural Steel Inventory

Structural steel industry material holding a high functional strength, especially standard items other than standard plate and few type of angle all other material type always depending customer demand. Material management function in structural steel industry listed as follows:-

Material Management common function in structural steel industry

1. Material Requirement Planning
2. Procurement Process
3. Shipping
4. Material Receiving, Storage, Material Issuance to Production, Scrap control

Material Requirement Planning

The main function of material requirement planning is to ensure the material availability on time either for production or direct to supply project site. The following are the major process involving in structural steel industry:

a. List the Material requirements
b. Check the general or on-hand stock
c. Prepare list of materials to be procured
d. Set-up and define process schedule for the materials

Procurement process

Structural steel procurement to be handled very systematically if you miss one section it may affect the delivery of steel to customer. To handle steel procurement for mass production to work with regular mills or supplier this will help to save cost as well as time schedule.

Procurement Process

a. Request for quotation
b. Opt procurement type
c. Purchase request process
d. Create shipping schedule
e. Purchase order process

Shipping

Shipping is one of the correlated functions of procurement, especially in structural steel procurement materials proper tracking and progress schedule time to time must maintain.

The below listed common function to clear the traffic:-

a. Progress monitoring
b. Schedule shipping

c. Organize Transport facility
d. Shipping documentation and verification
e. Custom clearance if foreign procurement
f. Materials shipping to warehouse

Material receiving, storage, issuance and control scrap

Materials has to receive against the MTC (Mill Test Certificate), has to store in right location and issuance has to execute according to the material requirements. The most important thing to issue and ensure to materials reached the right time for the production.

a. Incoming materials inspection
b. Materials segregation and store the materials in right location
c. Material physical issuance to production
d. Keep usable drops

MANUFACTURING

Manufacturing Functions

Structural steel manufacturing is the last stage of high process involved function of management. In manufacturing success is the key of the existence of structural steel business. A very high level of planning is must for the mass production type of business. For the entire manufacturing support the following function's integration is very important:

Production Planning & control

Production planning and control is the back born of structural steel manufacturing. To execute production there are many factors brings in to one pool for manufacturing like drawings, materials, CNC programs, cutting list, production support resource, production required consumables etc. has to bring together to the right time to the production location. While executing production there are many interruptions will encounter like priority change, revisions etc. all has to be managed without affecting the target. To organize production planning efficiently there are many other function's input and output details to be integrate and pump the information to production planning to do the right things in right time.

Manufacturing Preparation process

To support fabrication, preparation process of the manufacturing doing a major role. When a mass production location preparation process should organize by machines for different operation of the process like cutting, shape, drill, copying etc... preparation shop organization should done in-line the flow of operations to handle the materials efficiently. Efficiently to handle the preparation process, better investment and maintenance of machines is mandatory. As I mentioned earlier structural steel business is a time based formula, utilization of the time especially when it moves in production, construction group will be planning on other side for the erection of steel. So an hour delay of the any manufacturing process will affect the delivery. When you plan to invest in machines always look for ahead like machine efficiency, consumable part, technical support, machine maintenance etc. a proper plan will help to save cost, time and it will ensure your ROI.

Manufacturing fabrication process

Lay-out preparation, assembly, fit, welds most of the operation in this process executing manually even though some of the support can take from robotic control machines but since structural steel may not be standard type of product always, so this process efficiency all the case we believe in human resources. Shop organization should be in-line for the major process like station set-up for fit, inspection & weld it will help to save time in shop floor. Access of information should make it close or inside shop itself to do quick clarification like revision details, materials specially fitting components it will simplify and will support fabrication. Maintaining and availability of skilled and human resources is depending the efficiency of the product delivery of structural steel business.

Blasting / surface preparation process

According to the requirement of the project specification surface preparation has to be executed. There many automated machines and equipment are available, again as I stated in preparation process machines or equipment efficiency playing key role here also. Another thing when you do mass production materials handling and to ensure its identification that the entire steel component required for the particular rack gone through the process these are the challenging part of this process. That is material chasing and sent it through the process assurance and recording to be done time to time.

Painting / Galvanizing process

Structural steel coating according to project specification, coating type to be taken care, most of the companies internally doing painting application and sub-contracting galvanizing process. Painting process especially in structural steel there are different types of paints application using this is mainly depends the project location and climate. All the cases automation could not help in structural steel members all most all the cases here also depending skilled human resources.

Plant maintenance

Maintenance of machines / equipment of every industry have high importance to reduce idle or down time. Machine parts procurement and make the availability is one the important task then identifying the exact problem, method and efficiency in diagnosis the problem. Other part of the function is regular schedule for preventative maintenance.

Structural steel Fabrication sequences of activities

The following are the sequences of operations for structural steel fabrication

1. Cutting & machining
2. Punching & drilling
3. Straightening, bending and rolling
4. Fitting and reaming
5. Fastening (bolting, riveting and welding)
6. Surface treatment
7. Coating

Thanks to Mr. Zahiruddin Ahmed Operation Manager Indiana Steel who supported for structural steel fabrication sequences of activities. He was my colleague and works with Zamil Steel.

1. **Cutting & Machining**

Cutting to length is always the first process to be carried out, and this is done by any of the following methods

   a. Shearing and cropping

   Sections can be cut to length or width by cropping or shearing using CNC or hydraulic shears. Heavy sections or long plates can be shaped and cut to length by specialist plate shears. For smaller plates and sections, machines featuring a range of shearing knives, which can accept the differing section shapes, are available.

   b. Flame Cutting or Burning

   In this method, the steel is heated locally by a pressurized mixture of oxygen and a combustible gas such as propane, which passes through a ring of small holes in a cutting nozzle. The heat is focused on to a very narrow band and the steel melts when a jet of high-pressure oxygen is released through a separate hole in the centre of the nozzle to blast away the molten metal in globules. The desired cuts are obtained quickly by this process. However due to a rapid thermal cycle of heating and cooling, residual stresses and distortion are induced and hence structural sections that are fabricated using flame cutting are treated specially in the design of structural steelwork.

   c. Arc Plasma Cutting

   In this method, the cutting energy is produced electrically by heating a gas in an electric arc produced between a tungsten electrode and the work piece. This ionizes the gas, enabling it to conduct an electric current. The high-velocity plasma jet melts the metal of the work piece. The cut produced by plasma jet is very clean and its quality can be improved by using a water injection arc plasma torch. Plasma cutting is slow process.

   d. Cold Sawing

   When a section cannot be cut to length by cropping or shearing, then it is normally sawn. All saws for structural applications are mechanical and feature some degree of computer control. There are three forms of mechanical saw - circular, band and hack. The circular saw has a blade rotating in a vertical plane, which can cut either downwards or upwards, though the former is more common. Band saws have less capacity. Sections greater than *600 mm X 600 mm* cannot be sawn using band saws. The saw blade is a continuous metal edged, with cutting teeth, which is driven by an electric motor. Hack saws are mechanically driven reciprocating saws. They have normal format blades carried in a heavy duty hack saw frame. They have more productivity than band saws.

2. Punching and Drilling

Most fabrication shops have a range of machines, which can form holes for connections in structural steelwork. The traditional drilling machine is the radial drill, a manually operated machine, which drills individual holes in structural steelwork. But this method has become too slow for the primary line production. Therefore, larger fabricators have installed NC (Numerically Controlled) tooling, which registers and drills in response to keyed in data. These can drill many holes in flanges and webs of rolled steel sections simultaneously. It is also possible to punch holes, and this is particularly useful where square holes are specified such as anchor plates for foundation bolts. While this method is faster compared to drilling, punching creates distortion and material strain hardening around the holes, which increase with material thickness. Its use is currently restricted to smaller thickness plates. In order to reduce the effect of strain hardening and the consequent reduction in ductility of material around punched holes, smaller size (*2 mm* to *4 mm* lesser than final size) holes are punched and subsequently reamed to the desired size.

3. Straightening, Bending and Rolling

Rolled steel may get distorted after rolling due to cooling process. Further during transportation and handling operations, materials may bend or may even undergo distortion. This may also occur during punching operation. Therefore before attempting further fabrication the material should be straightened. In current practice, either rolls or gag presses are used to straighten structural shapes. Gag press is generally used for straightening beams, channels, angles, and heavy bars. This machine has a horizontal plunger or ram that applies pressure at points along the bend to bring it into alignment. Long plates, which are cambered out of alignment longitudinally, are frequently straightened by rollers. They are passed through a series of rollers that bend them back and forth with progressively diminishing deformation. Misalignments in structural shapes are sometimes corrected by spot or pattern heating. When heat is applied to a small area of steel, the larger unheated portion of the surrounding material prevents expansion. Upon cooling, the subsequent shrinkage produces a shortening of the member, thus pulling it back into alignment. This method is commonly employed to remove buckles in girder webs between stiffeners and to straighten members. It is frequently used to produce camber in rolled beams. A press brake is used to form angular bends in wide sheets and plates to produce cold formed steel members.

4. **Fitting and Reaming**

Before final assembly, the component parts of a member are fitted-up temporarily with rivets, bolts or small amount of welds. The fitting-up operation includes attachment of previously omitted splice plates and other fittings and the correction of minor defects found by the inspector.

In riveted or bolted work, especially when done manually, some holes in the connecting material may not always be in perfect alignment and small amount of reaming may be required to permit insertion of fasteners. The holes are reamed by electric or pneumatic reamers to the correct diameter, to produce well matched holes.

5. **Fastening Methods**

The strength of the entire structure depends upon the proper use of fastening methods. There are three methods of fastening namely bolting, riveting and welding. A few decades back, it was a common practice to assemble components in the workshop using bolts or rivets. Nowadays welding is the most common method of shop fabrication of steel structures. In addition to being simple to fabricate, welded connection considerably reduce the size of the joint and the additional fixtures and plates. However, there is still a demand for structural members to be bolted arising from a requirement to avoid welding because of the service conditions of the member under consideration. These may be low temperature performance criteria, the need to avoid welding stresses and distortion or the requirement for the component to be taken apart during service e.g. bolts in crane rails or bolted crane rails.

6. Finishing

Structural members whose ends must transmit loads by bearing against one another are usually finished to a smooth even surface. Finishing is performed by sawing, milling or other suitable means. Several types of sawing machines are available, which produce very satisfactory finished cuts. One type of milling machine employs a movable head fitted with one or more high-speed carbide tipped rotary cutters. The head moves over a bed, which securely holds the work piece in proper alignment during finishing operation. Bridge specifications require that sheared edges of plates over a certain thickness be edge planed. This is done to remove jagged flame cut edges and the residual stresses at the edges. In this operation, the plate is clamped to the bed of milling machine or a planer. The cutting head moves along the edge of the plate, planing it to a neat and smooth finish. The term finish or mill is used on detail drawings to describe any operation that requires steel to be finished to a smooth even surface by milling, planing, sawing or other machines.

7. Surface Treatment

Structural steelwork is protected against corrosion by applying metal or paint coating in the shop or at site.

Metal Coatings

The corrosion protection afforded by metallic coating largely depends upon the surface preparation, the choice of coating and its thickness. It is not greatly influenced by the method of application. Commonly used methods of applying metal coating to steel surfaces are hot-dip galvanizing & painting.

Galvanizing is the most common method of applying a metal coating to structural steelwork. In this method, the cleaned and fluxed steel is dipped in molten zinc. The steel reacts with molten zinc to form a series of zinc or iron alloys on its surface. As the steel work piece is removed, a layer of relatively pure zinc is deposited on top of the alloy layers. For most applications galvanized steel does not require painting.

An alternative method of applying metallic coating to structural steelwork is by metal spraying of either zinc or aluminum. The metal, in powder or wire form, is fed through a special spray gun containing a heat source, which can be either an oxy-gas flame or an electric arc. Molten globules of the metal are blown by a compressive jet on to the previously blast cleaned steel surface. No alloying occurs and the coating, which is produced, consists of porous overlapping platelets of metal. The pores are subsequently sealed, either by applying a thin organic coating which soaks into the surface, or by allowing the metal coating to weather, when corrosion products block the pores.

Paint Coatings

Painting is the principal method of protecting structural steelwork from corrosion. Paints are usually applied one coat on top of another, each coat having a specific function or use.

The primer is applied directly on to the cleaned steel surface. Its purpose is to wet the surface and to provide good adhesion for subsequently applied coats. Primers for steel surfaces are also usually required to provide corrosion inhibition. They are usually classified according to the main corrosion-inhibitive pigments used in their formulation, e.g. zinc phosphate, zinc chromate, red lead, and metallic-zinc. Each of these inhibitive pigments can be incorporated into a range of binder resins e.g. zinc phosphate alkyd primers, zinc phosphate epoxy primers, zinc phosphate chlorinated-rubber primers.

The intermediate coats (or undercoats) are applied to build the total film thickness of the system. This may involve application of several coats. The finishing coats provide the first-line defense against the environment and also determine the final appearance in terms of gloss, color etc. They also provide UV protection in exposed condition. Intermediate coats and finishing coats are usually classified according to their binders, e.g. vinyl finishes, urethane finishes.

The various superimposed coats within a painting system have, of course, to be compatible with one another. They may be all of the same generic type or may be different, e.g. chlor-rubber base intermediate coats that form a film by solvent evaporation and no oxidative process, may be applied on to an epoxy primer that forms a film by an oxidative process which involves absorption of oxygen from the atmosphere. However, as a first precaution, all paints within a system should normally be obtained from the same manufacturer.

Welding

Welding is used extensively for joining metals together and there is no doubt that it has been a most significant factor in the phenomenal growth of many industries.

A welded joint is made by fusing (melting) the steel plates or sections along the line of joint. The metal melted from each member of the joint unites in a pool of molten metal, which bridges the interface. As the pool cools, molten metal at the fusion boundary solidifies, forming a solid bond with the parent metal. When solidification completes, there is a continuity of metal through the joint.

There are five welding process regularly employed namely:

(i) Shielded Metal Arc Welding (SMAW)
(ii) Submerged-Arc Welding (SAW)
(iii) Manual Metal-Arc welding (MMA)
(iv) Metal-Active Gas welding (MAG)
(v) Stud welding
(vi) Flux Cored Arc Welding (FCAW)

Methods of welding

(1) Shielded Metal Arc Welding (SMAW)
This is basically a semi-automated or fully automated welding procedure. The type of welding electrode used would decide the weld properties. Since this welding is carried out under controlled condition, the weld quality is normally good.

(2) Submerged-Arc welding (SAW)
This is fully mechanized process in which the welding head is moved along the joint by a gantry, boom or tractor. The electrode is a bare wire, which is advanced by a motor. Here again, since the welding is carried out in controlled conditions, better quality welds are obtained.

(3) Manual Metal-Arc welding (MMA)
This is the most widely used arc welding process and appears to be advantageous

for labor intensive construction practices. As it is manually operated it requires considerable skill to produce good quality welds. Hence in the case of MMA, stringent quality control and quality assurance procedures are needed. Welders who are employed in actual fabrication are, in fact, graded according to their training and skills acquired.

(4) Metal-Active Gas welding (MAG)
This process is sometimes referred to as Metal-Inert Gas (MIG) welding. It is also manually operated. A gas that does not react with molten steel shields the arc and the weld pool. This protection ensures that a sound weld is produced free from contamination-induced cracks and porosity. Nevertheless, this procedure also depends on the skills of the welder.

(5) Stud welding
This is an arc welding process and is extensively used for fixing stud shear connectors to beam in the composite construction. The equipment consists of gun hand tool, D.C. power source, auxiliary contractor and controller. The stud is mounted into the chuck of the hand tool and conical tip of the stud is held in contact with the work piece by the pressure of a spring on the chuck. As soon as the current is switched on, the stud is moved away automatically to establish an arc. When a weld pool has been formed and the end of the stud is melted the latter is automatically forced into the steel plate and the current is switched off. The molten metal, which is expelled from the interface, is formed into a fillet by a ceramic collar or ferrule, which is placed around the stud at the beginning of the operation.

This process offers an accurate and fast method for attaching shear connectors, etc with the minimum distortion. While it requires some skill to set up the weld parameters (voltage, current, arc time and force), the operation of equipment is relatively straight forward.

(6) Flux Cored Arc Welding (FCAW)
The FCAW is a process in which coalescence is produced by heating with an electric arc between a continuous tubular consumable electrode and the work. The electrode is flux cored i.e. the flux is contained within the electrode which is hollow. In addition to flux, mineral and ferro alloys in the core can provide additional protection and composition control. The flux cored electrode is

coiled and supplied to the arc as a continuous wire as in CO_2 welding. The flux inside the wire provides the necessary shielding of the weld pool. Additional shielding may (or may not) be obtained from an externally supplied gas (e.g. CO_2) or gas mixture

Residual welding stresses

When a weld such as a butt weld is completed and begins to cool the hot weld and parent metal contracts longitudinally. The surrounding cold parent metal resists this contraction so that the weld is subjected to a tensile stress. This is balanced by the compressive stresses induced in the cold regions of the parent plate. These self-equilibrating forces introduce residual stresses both in the longitudinal and transverse direction. These stresses can even reach yield stress. Hence, the fabricator should adopt good fabrication practices that reduce the detrimental effect of residual stresses.

Butt welds
The welding sequence for double preparation has an important influence on the resultant distortion. If a few weld runs are first made on one side, and the plate turned over and then the same number of runs are made on the second side (i.e., sequential welding), a 'balanced' weld will be produced with little distortion. This will not, of course, be possible in situations where rotation of the plate is impracticable such as a plate, which is part of a large fabrication.

One aspect of butt-welding that should be noted is where back gouging is necessary to produce a full penetration weld. This can lead to distortion because the back gouging will produce bigger weld on the second side about the neutral axis of the plate. Such distortion can be reduced using an unsymmetrical weld section.

Fillet welds
In single and double fillets, shrinkage across the throat area can lead to distortion. The distortion caused by a double fillet weld is important in box or plate girder webs where stiffeners are attached to only one side of the web. The use of a thicker plate can reduce the fillet weld angular distortion due to increased stiffness.

Control of distortion

Some distortion from welding is due to transverse and longitudinal contraction of weldments. Adopting suitable methods that can resist contraction can control the distortion. Weld distortion of a flat plate with a series of stiffeners on one side can be countered by elastically prebending the plates. In a similar manner two T sections can be welded, prebent back to back, to prevent final curvature in the web plate.

Sometimes both presetting and prebending may be required, e.g. in plate girder fabrication where the web to flange welds are made automatically. When the welds are made manually, it is customary to put the stiffeners into the girder before the web/flange welds are made; in this way the square profile of the web to flange is maintained. Where automatic welding is employed the stiffeners cannot be put first since they would impede the progress of the automatic machine; in this presetting of the flange plates may be required. Welding should preferably be started at the centre of the fabrication and all succeeding welds from the centre outwards. This allows contraction to occur in the free condition. If the welding sequence is not chosen correctly, locked up stresses at either end of a welded portion can lead to uncorrectable distortions. Restraint procedure to reduce the effect of weld distortion should be carefully planned otherwise it can lead to solidification cracking.

Methods of correcting distortion

In general, there are two methods available to correct distortion namely:

a. applying force and
b. heating

Light sections can be corrected by applying force such as by hydraulic presses and local jacking or wedging. While heavier structures will require heating to apply stresses to reduce or eliminate the distortion. The effect of heating is similar to that of welding in which distortion results from the induced stresses. An area of steelwork will expand when heated but this expansion will be constrained by the surrounding cold unheated area, causing a plastic upset. On cooling, the area contracts and the element then becomes shorter, this principle can be used to correct or induce any curvature. The heat must be

evenly applied right through the material, if not, unwanted curvature may occur in the plan of the section. Rectangular heating across the bottom flange will shorten it compared with the top flange and hence induce camber. Since the shortening of the flange in the heated areas may tend to buckle the web adjacent to the flange, the heat is also applied to the web in a triangular manner such that the most affected part of the web contracts with the flange. In a similar manner a cambered plate may be straightened by applying triangular heating with the bases of the triangles parallel to the plate edges to be shortened. When the plate cools the heated edge will shorten and so reduce the camber. For panels in box girder webs, spot heating may be employed to reduce the concavity produced by the welding around the panel perimeter. Each spot contracts on cooling and induces a local plate shrinkage within the panel boundary and so reduces the dish. If the heat applied and the web panel thickness are such that there is a large temperature difference between the surfaces of the plate at each spot heat, then the resultant contraction on the hotter surface will produce a greater correction of the dish.

Defects in welds

Faulty welding procedure can lead to defects in the welds, thereby reducing the strength of the weld.

Some of the common defects in welds:

(i) Undercut
(ii) Porosity
(iii) Incomplete Penetration
(iv) Lack of side wall fusion
(v) Slag inclusions
(vi) cracks

It should be emphasised that a 'theoretical 100% error free' weld is not achievable in practice. While good quality welds are the priority of welders and weld inspectors, minor defects do normally creep in. Hence these defects are assessed during a weld inspection.

If the defects are within acceptable limits, they are accepted. If not, alternative measures of rectification may have to be carried out.

Nature of defects and their acceptability limits		
Nature of Defect	**Acceptance Norms**	**Disposition**
1. Crack, Lack of Fusion	Not accepted	Confirm by Magnetic Particle inspection, repair and retest.
2. Crater	Not accepted	Fill by weld deposit.
3. Undercut	Up to 0.8 mm accepted	Fill and grind smooth.
4. Porosity for butt or fillet welds	One pore of dia. <2.4mm every 100mm length is permitted. However pores of dia.>2.4mm not accepted	To be repair

QUALITY CONTROL

Quality control is a process employed to ensure a certain level of quality in a product or service. It may include whatever actions a business deems necessary to provide for the control and verification of certain characteristics of a product or service. The basic goal of quality control is to ensure that the products, services, or processes provided meet specific requirements and are dependable, satisfactory, and fiscally sound.

Essentially, quality control involves the examination of a product, service, or process for certain minimum levels of quality. The goal of a quality control team is to identify products or services that do not meet a company's specified standards of quality. If a problem is identified, the job of a quality control team or professional may involve stopping production temporarily. Depending on the particular service or product, as well as the type of problem identified, production or implementation may not cease entirely.

Usually, it is not the job of a quality control team or professional to correct quality issues. Typically, other individuals are involved in the process of discovering the cause of quality issues and fixing them. Once such problems are overcome, the product, service, or process continues production or implementation as usual.

Quality control Focus in structural steel industry

The following are the some of the main focus need to giving quality control for structural steel industries:

a. Interpretation of conformance to customers quality requirements
b. Review of customer drawings and specifications
c. Determination of necessary inspection points
d. Documentation of necessary inspection and test instructions and changes thereto
e. Planning, developing, initiating, coordinating, implementing and maintaining the most effective and efficient procedures for quality assurance
f. Maintenance of adequate quality assurance records
g. Conduct in house audit
h. Conduct quality standards audit for vendors
i. Assist customer audit and inspections
j. Maintenance of adequate quality assurance records
k. Review of quality assurance and corrective action follow-up
l. Vendor quality assurance and corrective action follow-up
m. Original and continuing periodic inspection of special and standard gages, test equipment, and tooling used to manufacture product. Assuring inspection and test equipment remain calibrated within established time
n. Coordinate in plant corrective action on items rejected by the customer, notify customer of the action taken and evaluate the action for effectiveness
o. Assure that inspection personnel are capable of rendering are unbiased decision to accept or reject material inspected
p. Initiate concise written work instructions for the acceptance or rejection of a product
q. Review purchase orders against the delivery

Process inspection stages

Inspection process in structural steel not limited to a particular stage some of the important process which is unavoidable to maintain the quality of the structural steel product

   a. Incoming raw material inspection
   b. Welding consumable
   c. Preparation process inspection
   d. Fit-up process inspection
   e. Welding process inspection
   f. Surface preparation stage inspection
   g. Coating process inspection
   h. Packing process inspection

Quality control in fabrication

Quality assurance during fabrication assumes utmost importance in ensuring that the completed structure behaves in the manner envisaged during design stage. Any deviation from these design considerations as reflected in detail drawings may introduce additional stresses to the structure and affect its strength and durability. This section discusses the relevant aspects in fabrication and erection, which need to be considered to achieve the desired quality.

Fabrication
A fabricator's work starts from the point of procurement of raw materials including fasteners and ends with the dispatch of the fabricated items to site for erection.

In order to ensure that the fabrication can be carried out in accordance with the drawings, it is necessary that inspection and checking is carried out in accordance with an agreed Quality Assurance Plan (QAP). The plan should elaborate on checks and inspections of the raw materials and also of the components as they are fabricated, joined etc.

Imperfections in Fabrication
Structural steelwork cannot be fabricated to exact dimensions and some degree of imperfection is bound to occur during fabrication process. The limits of various imperfections are spelt out in the specifications. In the design, these

are accounted by adopting a factor of safety for material. However, in some components an increase of imperfection beyond these limits may lead to reduction in the strength and durability of the structure e.g., imperfections on the straightness of the individual flanges of a rolled beam or a fabricated girder results in the reduction of strength of the girder due to lateral torsional buckling which may cause an overall bow in the girder. This, in turn, may generate twisting moments at the supports.

As a rule all columns and struts should be checked for straightness on completion of fabrication. Also, all rolled and fabricated girders should be checked over a distance in the longitudinal direction equal to the depth of the section in the region and points of concentrated load.

Making holes
Excessive cold working of structural steel can cause reduction in ductility, embrittlement and cracking. Punching holes is a cold-working operation and can, therefore, cause brittle fracture. This becomes critical for the durability of structures subjected to fluctuation of stresses such as railway bridges and crane girders. Under cyclic loading fatigue cracks can initiate from such punched holes. In such cases, holes for bolts may be formed either by drilling or by punching undersize holes followed by reaming to desired size. Drilling is preferable to punching, because it reduces the chances of brittle fracture. Studies show that punching may produce short cracks extending radially from the hole, thereby enhancing the possibility of initiating brittle fracture at the hole when the member is loaded. Even in statically loaded structures the maximum thickness of plates in which holes can be punched is restricted.

Shop assembly and camber check
During this operation, the overall dimensions of the structure including alignment, squareness, camber etc. should be confirmed. Inadequate or erroneous camber, in fact, introduces huge secondary stresses in the members instead of eliminating these as originally desired. Shop assembly also ensures that the open holes drilled in various units are within tolerable limits.

Welded joints
As presented in the previous sections, welded joints are very important as far as the quality control of the joints is concerned. It is well known that joints are

the last straw of strength in structural steelwork. Any poor quality weld would detrimentally affect the joint and in turn affect the performance of the whole structure itself. Hence welded joints need thorough inspection during and after the fabrication. Different methods of Non-Destructive Testing (NDT) and evaluation of welds are available.

MAJOR CHALLENGE OR CONSTRAINTS OF OPERATIONS

In structural steel business operation there are many constraints the listed are the some of the common in day to day operations of the business.

a. Raw-material specially (particular steel section) fabricators has to wait rolling schedule in case if it is not regular
b. Steel price
c. Shipping delay
d. Fabrication (shop) drawing readiness for the fabrication schedule
e. Revisions during various stage of fabrication
f. Fabrication complexity
g. Process inspection
h. Skilled man-power
i. Production priority change
j. Storage
k. Transportations

IT ROLE FOR STRUCTURAL STEEL BUSINESS

Structural steel mass production platform IT is playing unavoidable role to support the business day to day activity. Most of the case structural steel main processes are measuring in terms of time against the weight as measuring point. Resources organization and ensure its right utilization in right time is major challenge of structural steel business. Let us see the major IT support required functions for structural steel business.

a. Estimation management
- Enquiry Scope defining module
- Cost estimate structure
- Quotation preparation

b. Project Management
- Contract administration
- Scope confirmation
- Communication management
- Claim management
- Costing & billing

c. Project Planning
- Process defining and schedule
- Expedition management
- Tracking & Reports

d. Purchasing
- Enquiry
- Quotation Analysis
- Contract Management
- Purchase Order
- Shipping

e. Materials Management
- Material Requirement Planning
- Material Receiving
- Material Management & control
- Material issuance

f. Production Planning and Resources Planning
- Production resources planning
- Production process schedule
- Production order issuance
- Material Requirement issuance
- Expedition
- Shop floor Track & control
- Revision or modification management

g. QC Inspection Module
- Process Inspection Module
- Finishing Inspection Module

h. Shipping & Logistics Management
- Packing modules
- Transportation Booking & Schedule
- Physical Loading confirmation
- Material Delivery
- Invoicing & Tax

CONCLUSION

In this book I am sharing my experience of structural steel industry and I feel that even though there are some complications in operation but a well-organized and integrated platform of structural steel business can make long future. I want to emphasis structural steel manufactures to have an integrated management system is essential to manage and control structural steel business day to day operation and will add to the project revenue.

www.ingramcontent.com/pod-product-compliance
Lightning Source LLC
Chambersburg PA
CBHW021036180526
45163CB00005B/2156